HEINEMA

LEARN TO
KEYBOARD

SHARON SPENCER

the quick and easy way

Heinemann Educational Publishers,
Halley Court, Jordan Hill, Oxford OX2 8EJ
A division of Reed Educational & Professional Publishing Ltd

Heinemann is a registered trademark of Reed Educational & Professional Publishing Limited

OXFORD MELBOURNE AUCKLAND JOHANNESBURG BLANTYRE GABORONE IBADAN
PORTSMOUTH NH (USA) CHICAGO

First published 1999
2002 2001 2000 99
10 9 8 7 6 5 4 3 2 1

A catalogue record for this book is available from the British Library on request.

ISBN 0 435 45380 7

Designed by Natasha Goddard and Sarah Garbett

Typeset by TechType, Abingdon, Oxon

Printed in Scotland by Thomson Litho Ltd

Acknowledgements

I would like to thank all those who helped in the preparation
of this book, particularly Rosalyn Bass and Natasha Goddard
at Heinemann Educational for their advice and
encouragement. I would also like to thank Joseph for trialling
the scheme and Ian and Lucy for their support while writing
this book.

Tel:01865 888058 email:info.he@heinemann.co.uk

Contents

Contents

Introduction

About this book

This book is the essential guide for anyone who wants to learn how to key quickly and accurately. The exercises throughout the book ensure your fingers are in the right place and you are encouraged to key in using both hands working together as soon as possible.

Each page gives you the opportunity to practice keys already learnt, followed by new keys, and a chance to apply your new skills by keying in words and sentences. You can practise each line as many times as you need to until the movements feel comfortable and the keys are familiar.

The keyboard diagram at the top of each page highlights the new keys to be learnt so you know exactly where to find them when keying in. You will also find tips on each page which are well worth taking note of.

Once you have mastered the skills of keyboarding you can practise keying in your own documents, including letters and memos to prepare you for the world of work.

Learning to keyboard

The aim of this book is to teach you how to 'touch keyboard' – being able to keyboard quickly without looking at the keys.

The important thing to remember when learning to keyboard is to check that you have placed your fingers on the home keys (see page 7) especially when learning a new key. Once you are sure your fingers are in the correct position, you should try to keep your eyes on the book. Concentrate on your accuracy to begin with and your speed will be built up over a period of time. It may help if you say the name of the key you are striking.

Try to practise every day, even if it is only for a few minutes. Ten minutes of concentrated effort on a regular basis is of far more use than one hour twice a week. Short bursts of regular effort will help you build your keyboarding skills.

Before you start keyboarding

Posture

Before you start keyboarding, make sure you are sitting correctly. If you follow these basic rules you can avoid any kind of strain injury.

- You should be sitting with your feet firmly on the floor and your back straight.
- Sit facing the keyboard with both your body and the keyboard in a straight line.
- The keyboard should be fairly near the end of the desk or table.
- Your wrists should not touch the desk or lean on the keyboard.

Paper sizes

When printing your work, the most common paper sizes are A4 and A5.

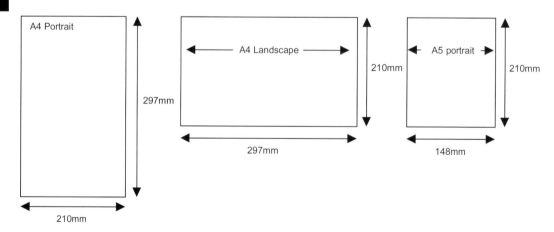

You will need to learn the measurements of these so that you can work out

- how much space you have left on a page
- how much space to allocate for margins etc

Setting margins

Most word processing programs are preset with the following margins as the default setting.

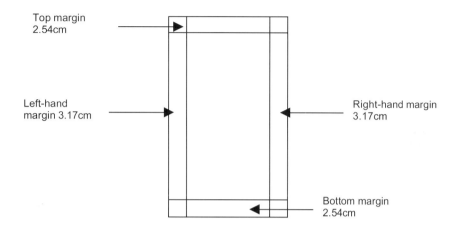

Top margin 2.54cm

Left-hand margin 3.17cm

Right-hand margin 3.17cm

Bottom margin 2.54cm

These default settings are acceptable for all the documents you produce. If you want to change the default setting, it is usual to leave a margin of 2.5cm for the left and right margins as well as at the top and bottom of the page.

Fonts

This piece of text is typed in a font called Palatino. There are many different fonts available on word processing programs. You may have some interesting fonts available, but remember, your aim in word processing is to produce work that is clear and easy to read! Fancy fonts are best left for posters and design work.

The most common fonts and sizes for keyboarding are:

- Times New Roman – size 12

- Arial – size 10 or 11

You will notice that each letter takes up a different amount of space. This is called 'proportional spacing' and means that each letter uses only the space that it needs. For example, a capital W will take up more room than a capital I. Depending on the font and font size you use for the drills which follow, your line lengths will almost certainly differ from those in this book.

Using the return key

It is important that you know how to move to the next line. To do this you press the 'return' key. This is the key at the right-hand side of the keyboard that looks like this:

You do not usually need to press the return key each time you wish to move to a new line as word processors will automatically move to a new line when you have reached the right hand margin. This is called 'text wrap'. However, when learning to keyboard you will need to start a fresh line for each drill by pressing the return key at the end of each line.

Line spacing

The default setting for line spacing on most word processing packages is single line spacing. This means that each line will be immediately below the previous line. For ease of proof reading it is a good idea to use one-and-a-half line spacing or double line spacing for the keyboarding drills that follow. You will need to find out how to set this spacing in your word processing package.

When producing your own documents, the important thing is to ensure you use consistent line spacing.

Correcting errors

When you are learning to keyboard it is better not to correct errors. You will need to be able to see the mistakes you make most often so that you can give these keys extra practice.

Keyboarding

Home keys With both hands, find the home keys as shown below. Your fingers should hover above these key at all times. The home keys are **A S D F** (left hand) and **J K L ;** (right hand). These keys are highlighted on the keyboard below. Finding the 'home keys' means that your fingers can find their way around the keyboard. They are like a familiar landmark – as soon as you have spotted it, you can find your way home easily!

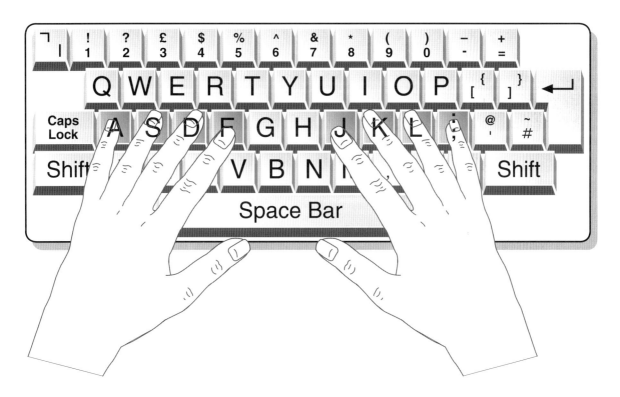

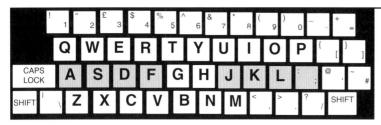

Left hand

A S D F

Right hand

J K L ;

Tip	Try keyboarding the following home keys, saying the keys as you type them and trying to build up a rhythm. Remember to use the correct fingers.

Use your thumb, it doesn't matter which, to press the space bar between each set of letters. There is no need to press the space bar at the end of each line as you will then press the return key.

Use your little finger to press the return key at the end of each line.

Remember to practise each line as many times as you need until you feel comfortable using the keys.

Practise home keys

```
asdf ;lkj asdf ;lkj asdf ;lkj asdf ;lkj asdf ;lkj asdf
fdsa jkl; fdsa jkl; fdsa jkl; fdsa jkl; fdsa jkl; fdsa
afaf ;j;j afaf ;j;j fafa j;j; fafa j;j; afaf ;j;j afaf
adad ;k;k adad ;k;k dada k;k; dada k;k; adad ;k;k adad
asas ;l;l asas ;l;l sasa l;l; sasa l;l; asas ;l;l asas
sfsf ljlj sfsf ljlj fsfs jljl fsfs jljl sfsf ljlj sfsf
sdsd lklk sdsd lklk dsds klkl dsds klkl sdsd lklk sdsd
dfdf kjkj dfdf kjkj fdfd jkjk fdfd jkjk dfdf kjkj dfdf
asdf ;lkj asdf ;lkj asdf ;lkj asdf ;lkj asdf ;lkj asdf
fdsa jkl; fdsa jkl; fdsa jkl; fdsa jkl; fdsa jkl; fdsa
asdf ;lkj asdf ;lkj asdf ;lkj asdf ;lkj asdf ;lkj asdf
fdsa jkl; fdsa jkl; fdsa jkl; fdsa jkl; fdsa jkl; fdsa
afaf ;j;j afaf ;j;j fafa j;j; fafa j;j; afaf ;j;j afaf
```

Left hand

Right hand

| **Tip** | Print out your practice so far. Circle and make a note of any letters you got wrong. |

Review home keys

```
asdf  ;lkj  fdsa  jkl;  a;sl  dkfj  fjdk  sla;  asdf  ;lkj  fdsa

sad;  fad;  add;  dad;  sad;  fad;  add;  dad;  sad;  fad;  add;

asdf  ;lkj  fdsa  jkl;  a;sl  dkfj  fjdk  sla;  asdf  ;lkj  fdsa

sad;  fad;  add;  dad;  sad;  fad;  add;  dad;  sad;  fad;  add;
```

Practise both hands together

```
a;a;  ;a;a  alal  lala  akak  kaka  ajaj  jaja  a;a;  ;a;a  alal

s;s;  ;s;s  slsl  lsls  sksk  ksks  sjsj  jsjs  s;s;  ;s;s  slsl

d;d;  ;d;d  dldl  ldld  dkdk  kdkd  djdj  jdjd  d;d;  ;d;d  dldl

f;f;  ;f;f  flfl  lflf  fkfk  kfkf  fjfj  jfjf  f;f;  ;f;f  flfl

a;a;  ;a;a  alal  lala  akak  kaka  ajaj  jaja  a;a;  ;a;a  alal

s;s;  ;s;s  slsl  lsls  sksk  ksks  sjsj  jsjs  s;s;  ;s;s  slsl

d;d;  ;d;d  dldl  ldld  dkdk  kdkd  djdj  jdjd  d;d;  ;d;d  dldl

f;f;  ;f;f  flfl  lflf  fkfk  kfkf  fjfj  jfjf  f;f;  ;f;f  flfl
```

Apply the keys you know

```
lad;  fad;  add;  sad;  dad;  all;  ask;  lass;  fall;  lads;

dads;  asks;  flask;  salad;  flak;  alas;  dada;  daff;  lad;

ask;  lass;  flask;  lad;  fad;  lad;  add;  sad;  dad;  fall;

lads;  dads;  flask;  jaffa;  flak;  all;  ask;  lass;  ask;

lass;  flask;  jaffa;  daff;  lad;  fad;  add;  sad;  dad;  all;
```

| Tip | Remember to concentrate on accuracy when learning the keyboard. |

Review home keys

```
asdf ;lkj fdsa jkl; asdf ;lkj fdsa jkl; asdf ;lkj fdsa
flask; salad; alas; adds; asks; lass; flask; salad;
a lad asks dad; alas a lass asks dad; a lad asks dad;
dads; asks; flask; salad; flak; all; ask; lass; lass;
flask; dada; daff;
```

Practise new keys

```
ghgh hghg ghgh hghg ghgh hghg ghgh hghg ghgh hghg ghgh
ahah ;h;h shsh lhlh dhdh khkh fhfh jhjh agag ;g;g sgsg
lglg dgdg kgkg fgfg jgjg ahah ;h;h shsh lhlh dhdh khkh
fhfh jhjh agag ;g;g sgsg lglg dgdg kgkg fgfg jgjg ahah
;h;h shsh lhlh dhdh khkh fhfh jhjh agag ;g;g sgsg lglg
dgdg kgkg fgfg jgjg ahah ;h;h shsh lhlh dhdh khkh fhfh
jhjh agag ;g;g sgsg lglg dgdg kgkg fgfg jgjg ahah ;h;h
shsh lhlh dhdh khkh fhfh jhjh agag ;g;g sgsg lglg dgdg
```

Apply the keys you know

```
had; sag; gas; lag; jag; hag; add; has; had; sag; gas;
dad has had a jaffa; alas lads shall fall; a glad dash;
lass falls as lads dash; slash a jaffa; salad; flask;
```

Word groupings

```
shall hall gall fall shall hall gall fall gall shall
slash lash ash gash dash flash slash lash gash slash
```

Y Use the **J** finger

T Use the **F** finger

Tip Remember to practise each line as many times as you need to until you feel comfortable using the keys.

Review keys

asdf ;lkj ghgh hghg ag;h sglh dgkh fgjh had; sag; gas;

aha; gad; gag; gaff; ghat; glad; half; hash; lash;

salad; flask; jaffa; glass; had; sag; gas; lag; jag;

hag; add; has; falls; has; lads; dash; gaff; ghat;

Practise new keys

tyty ytyt tyty ytyt tyty ytyt tyty ytyt tyty ytyt tyty

ayay ;t;t sysy ltlt dydy ktkt fyfy jtjt gygy htht atat

;y;y stst lyly dtdt kyky ftft jyjy gtgt hyhy ayay ;t;t

sysy ltlt dydy ktkt fyfy jtjt gygy htht atat ;y;y stst

lyly dtdt kyky ftft jyjy gtgt hyhy ayay ;t;t sysy ltlt

Apply the keys you know

jay; hat; tag; hay; lay; gay; day; say; yak; ash; halt;

tall; talk; data; dash; last; fast; aghast; sky; stay;

salad; allay; dastardly; stag; staff; talk; a daft yak;

that ghastly stag; staff talk fast; halt dastardly fly;

a tall lad halts at a stall; say all jaffas fall;

Word groupings

hay lay gay day say stay jay slay flay hay lay gay day

hat sat flat fat slat that hat sat flat fat slat that

V Use the **F** finger

B Use the **F** finger

N Use the **J** finger

Tip Remember to return your finger to the **F** key immediately after you have stretched over to key in the letter **B**.

Review keys

asdf ;lkj alks skj; djsk gajl tjah last; fast; aghast;

sky; stay; lay; gay; day; hall; fall; tall; gall;

gaga; gala; half; gash; dash; sash; lash; saga; flask;

salad; alaska; jaffa; flash; add; dad; sad; fad; add;

Practise new keys

vnvn vbvb nbnb nvnv bvbv vnvn bvbv nbvn vnvn vbvb nbnb

avsv ;nln dvfv knjn absb ;vlv kvfv kvjv anan ;n;n snsn

lnln dndn knkn fnfn jnjn gngn hnhn tntn ynyn ;v;v avav

lvlv svsv kvkv dvdv jvjv fvfv hvhv gvgv yvyv tvtv abab

;b;b sbsb lblb dbdb kbkb fbfb jbjb gbgb hbhb tbtb ybyb

anan ;n;n snsn lnln dndn knkn fnfn jnjn gngn hnhn tntn

ynyn ;v;v avav lvlv svsv kvkv dvdv jvjv fvfv hvhv gvgv

Apply the keys you know

slant; sandal; bang; stand; fang; land; gang; hand;

gang; gland; gnat; abash; baby; bald; ball; bank; ant;

natal; nasty; nasal; vast; blandly; java; flan;

navy; vary; vastly; bat; bats; bank; stank; blank;

slant; sandal; bang; stand; fang; land; gang; hand;

Word groupings

sand land band bland hand stand gland sand land band

bang hang fang sang gang stang bang hang fang sang gang

12

 SHIFT Use the **A** finger or the **;** finger

. Use the **L** finger

| **Tip** | Once you start typing sentences, you do not need to press the return key at the end of each line – the text will flow from line to line automatically. Remember, the number of words you can fit on a line may not be the same as in this book as you may be using a different font and font size. |

Shift key

Use either the right or left shift key to make a capital letter. Hold down the shift key with your little finger and type the required letter. Use the **A** finger for the left shift key and the **:** finger for the right shift key. Release the shift key after typing the capital letter.

Full stop

Use the **L** finger to type the full stop. Leave, either one or two spaces after a full stop – but make sure you are consistent. That is, *always* use one space or *always* use two spaces.

Practise new keys

```
aAss  dDff  ;jLL  kKjJ  a.s.  ;.l.  d.f.  k.j.  A.S.  L.K.  D.J.
a.a.  ;.;.  s.s.  l.l.  d.d.  k.k.  f.f.  j.j.  g.g.  h.h.  t.t.
y.y.  v.v.  n.n.  b.b.  A.A.  ;.;.  S.S.  L.L.  D.D.  K.K.  F.F.
J.J.  G.G.  H.H.  T.T.  Y.Y.  V.V.  N.N.  B.B.  a.a.  ;.;.  s.s.
l.l.  d.d.  k.k.  f.f.  j.j.  g.g.  h.h.  t.t.  y.y.  v.v.  n.n.
b.b.  A.A.  ;.;.  S.S.  L.L.  D.D.  K.K.  F.F.  J.J.  G.G.  H.H.
T.T.  Y.Y.  V.V.  N.N.  B.B.  a.a.  ;.;.  s.s.  l.l.  d.d.  k.k.
```

Practise new keys

```
Ask Val. Dad has a hat. A bad task. Jan has a bag. Dad
asks Jan. Dan had a gang. Ask Kay and Tasha. Bats fly
and hang at a slant. A band sang at a flash bandstand.
Hans has a van. Stall Yan and ask Dad and Sanjay.
```

Word groupings

```
Brag. Brad. Brat. Bran. Brand. Brass. Brag. Brands.
Stan. Stand. Staff. Stall. Stay. Stab. Stag. Stands.
```

Tip | Remember to practice each line as many times as you need until you feel comfortable using the keys

Review keys

lfka jd;s fla; sljd jskf d;al kdaf jl;s lfka jd;s fla;

Gang; gland; gnat; abash; baby; bald; ball; Gang;

Balsa: blank: van: vandal: navy: natal: nasal: nab:

nag. gaga. gala. half. gash. dash. sash. lash. saga.

Practise new keys

ruru urur ruru urur ruru urur ruru urur ruru urur ruru

arsr drfr ;ulu kuju ausu dufu ;rlr krjr ruas ru;l kuar

auau ;u;u susu lulu dudu kuku fufu juju gugu huhu tutu

yuyu vuvu nunu bubu .u.u arar ;r;r srsr lrlr drdr krkr

frfr jrjr grgr hrhr trtr yryr vrvr nrnr brbr .r.r auau

;u;u susu lulu dudu kuku fufu juju gugu huhu tutu yuyu

vuvu nunu bubu .u.u arar ;r;r srsr lrlr drdr krkr frfr

jrjr grgr hrhr trtr yryr vrvr nrnr brbr .r.r auau ;u;u

Apply the keys you know

Ruth has sunburn. Ruby runs fast. Jay had a runny flan.

Fay had a ball. Saul taught a lad and lass. Ruby and

Ruth rush a task. Rufus unfurls a band. Ask Barry and

Janus. Ruth has sunburn. Ruby runs fast.

Word groupings

taught haughty naughty fraught taught naughty haughty

last fast vast blast aghast ghastly last vast blast

C Use the **D** finger

M Use the **J** finger

Tip When you have finished keyboarding the drills, check them carefully to see if you have made any mistakes.

Review keys

asdf ;lkj ghty bnvr tygh jfty abdg nthg nab: dash.
Stud; suds; rang; rank; runt; sulk; Sung; stud; such;
rush; stunt; stuff; Stunk; sunny; rusty; stylus; sash.
sturdy; Balsa: blank: van: vandal: navy: natal: nasal:

Practise new keys

cmcm mcmc cmcm mcmc cmcm mcmc cmcm mcmc cmcm mcmc cmcm
acsc dcfc ;mlm kmjm amsm dmfm ;clc kcjc acjc lmfm scml
acac ;c;c scsc lclc dcdc kckc fcfc jcjc gcgc hchc tctc
ycyc vcvc ncnc bcbc .c.c rcrc ucuc amam ;m;m smsm lmlm
dmdm kmkm fmfm jmjm gmgm hmhm tmtm ymym vmvm nmnm bmbm
.m.m rmrm umum acac ;c;c scsc lclc dcdc kckc fcfc jcjc
gcgc hchc tctc ycyc vcvc ncnc bcbc .c.c rcrc ucuc amam
;m;m smsm lmlm dmdm kmkm fmfm jmjm gmgm hmhm tmtm ymym
vmvm nmnm bmbm .m.m rmrm umum acac ;c;c scsc lclc dcdc

Apply the keys you know

Murray caught a ball. Jay ran and ran. At Ramadan
Sanjay fasts. Mary can carry a rucksack and a handbag.
Dan and Harry could ask Mum. Jay has muddy sandals and
sunburnt arms. A ghastly drama unfurls. Murray caught a
ball. Jay ran and ran. At Ramadan Sanjay fasts.

Word groupings

arm alarm farm harm karma barmy alarm farm harm arm
art start tart dart cart Bart arty dart start tart

E Use the **D** finger

I Use the **K** finger

| Tip | Try to keep your fingers hovering above the home keys rather than allowing your fingers to rest on them. |

Review keys

asdf ;lkj ucma rtnm lrty ashj unc; vrka scsc dcdc fcfc

Carry; car; cart; cam; call; macadam; Mack; mad;

macula; madly; madrigal; Magma; Magna Carta; magnate;

mural; Murmur; muscat; mug; mull; mark;

Practise new keys

eiei ieie eiei ieie eiei ieie eiei ieie eiei ieie eiei

aese defe ;ili kiji aisi difi ;ele keje kedi jeki fjie

aeae ;e;e sese lele dede keke fefe jeje gege hehe tete

yeye veve nene bebe .e.e rere ueue cece meme aiai ;i;i

sisi lili didi kiki fifi jiji gigi hihi titi yiyi vivi

nini bibi .i.i riri uiui cici mimi aeae ;e;e sese lele

Apply the keys you know

The Inland Revenue visited me. Rick had an injured ear.
He ate beans and drunk juice. Henry takes the minutes
at the meeting. Having this flu is very debilitating.
Ben and Indy hid under the stairs. Jack caught them.
The Inland Revenue visited me. Rick had an injured ear.

Word groupings

Deed feed greed heed need reed seed indeed seedless
End bend send fend lend mend trend friend tend rend
Bess less mess guess Jess Tess necessary message

Speed and Accuracy Drills

It is important that you can key in at speed. However, it is equally important that you can key in accurately. In order to improve both, you will need to practise for a few minutes each day. You will soon see your speed increasing.

Measured speed is tested in 'typing words'. Every five characters equals a word. These include punctuation and the spaces between words and after punctuation. For example, a sentence that contains 60 characters would have 12 'typing words'.

Building your speed is hard work, but very rewarding.

In order to test your speed and accuracy try the following:

1   Key in the speed and accuracy drills carefully, concentrating on your accuracy. The speed of your keying in is not important. Aim for 100% accuracy.

2   Once you have checked your work for errors, key in the drill again, as quickly as you can, allowing yourself one minute to complete it. If you manage to complete the drill in this time, then go back to the beginning and carry on keying in.

        Check your work carefully, stopping at the second error. The number of 'typing words' you have keyed in up to the point of the second error is the number of words you can key in within a minute. Remember that each 'typing word' is five characters (including spaces and punctuation).

Aim to key in each drill in one minute with no more than two errors

Daniel and Anne are having a kitchen fitted early next year. (12 words per minute)

Richard has a birthday in August. He shall be thirty three. (12 words per minute)

X Use the **S** finger

, Use the **K** finger

| Tip | Use the letter x (lower case) for the word *by* – e.g. 10 mm x 97 mm. |

Review keys

asdf ;lkj g;tl fkey uric rbmj yesc ndef scsc dcdc fcfc

Made; mead; ride; feed; side; ride; tide; bide; hide;

earn; learn; fern; dream; team; lean; keen; mean; seen;

Practise new keys

x,x, ,x,x x,x, ,x,x x,x, ,x,x x,x, ,x,x x,x,

axsx dxfx ;,l, k,j, a,s, d,f, ;xlx kxjx jxd, k,dx ax,j

axax ;x;x sxsx lxlx dxdx kxkx fxfx jxjx gxgx hxhx txtx

yxyx vxvx nxnx bxbx .x.x rxrx uxux cxcx mxmx exex ixix

a,a, ;,;, s,s, l,l, d,d, k,k, f,f, j,j, g,g, h,h, t,t,

y,y, v,v, n,n, b,b, .,., r,r, u,u, c,c, m,m, e,e, i,i,

Apply the keys you know

Reg exited the exam hall feeling excited, lucky and relieved. Extend the right arm carefully, then bend the knees. The farmer held his axe tightly, he listened carefully, then he let it fall. Xmas is here again.

Word groupings

Air, fair, hair, lair, stair, hairdresser, flair, airs.
Light, might, fight, tight, right, sight, night, blight

Speed and accuracy drills

Aim to key in each drill in one minute with no more than two errors

This century has seen many changes. The greatest may be the advance of IT. 15 words a minute

The hairdresser was on a tight schedule. Three clients needed their hair dried. 16 words a minute

W Use the **S** finger

O Use the **L** finger

Tip Remember to key the speed and accuracy drill twice – once for accuracy and once for speed and accuracy.

Review keys

axcm nxc, rmek ibun sevb ;iun glxi ygnj Axis, axle, biaxial, beeswax, extent, Extricate, exult, exude, extreme, Exterminate, extensive, exercise, extra

Practise new keys

wowo owow wowo owow wowo owow wowo owow wowo owow wowo
awsw ;olo dwfw kojo aoso dofo ;wlw awaw ;w;w swsw lwlw
dwsw kwkw fwfw jwjw gwgw hwhw twtw ytyt vwvw nwnw bwbw
.w.w rwrw uwuw cwcw mwmw ewew iwiw xwxw ,w,w aoao ;o;o
soso lolo dodo koko fofo jojo gogo hoho toto yoyo vovo
nono bobo .o.o roro uouo coco momo eoeo ioio xoxo ,o,o

Apply the keys you know

Will you write a letter for me to the manager of Forward Clothes Ltd. Thank you. When I want to wander in the woods, I will make sure I tell you first.

Word groupings

Able, suitable, reliable, available, extractable.
Let, bet, get, jet, met, pet, set, vet, wet, yet, net.
Look, cook, book, hook, rook, took, shook, crook, took.

Speed and accuracy drills

Aim to key in each drill in one minute with no more than two errors

Working from home is becoming more common these days. It makes sense. <u>14 words per minute</u>
Learning to keyboard can be hard work but the effort you make will soon show good results. <u>18 words per minute</u>

CAPS LOCK

Use the **A** finger

Caps lock

The caps lock is the larger key directly above the shift key. When you press this key, any characters you key in afterwards will be in capitals.

Where two symbols appear on a key, the symbol on the lower half of the key can be keyed in when the *caps lock key* is being used – for example, the full stop and the comma.

When the *caps lock key* is being used only the numbers shown on the figure row can be keyed in – not the symbols.

You always need to use the *shift key* to key in the symbols on the figure row and those on the upper half of keys with two symbols.

Remember: The *caps lock key* needs to be pressed again to return to lower-case letters.

Try using the caps lock on the following drills:

SHUT THE DOOR when you leave.

DO NOT RUN in the swimming area.

NO SMOKING in the office.

The sign stated DO NOT WALK ON THE GRASS.

JANICE, MICHAEL and ROBERT are the winners.

The contest starts on TUESDAY.

The notice stated NO DOGS in the park.

SWITCH OFF your mobile when entering the building.

Tip	Do the speed and accuracy drills twice – once for accuracy and once for speed and accuracy.

Review keys	asdf ;lkj xiem ,gho ruvn bcty wox, judv Witch, which, ordinary, whereabouts, Wise, wisdom, warthog, orange, olive, Orlando, with, what, would when, will, gaga;

Practise new keys	z.z. .z.z z.z. .z.z z.z. .z.z z.z. .z.z z.z. .z.z z.z. azsz dzfz ;.l. k.j. a.s. d.f. ;zlz kzjz f.kz dzj. a.zj a.a. ;.;. s.s. l.l. d.d. k.k. f.f. j.j. g.g. h.h. t.t. y.y. v.v. n.n. b.b. r.r. u.u. c.c. m.m. e.e. i.i. x.x. ,.,. w.w. o.o. azaz ;z;z szsz lzlz dzdz kzkz fzfz jzjz gzgz hzhz tztz yzyz vzvz nznz bzbz .z.z rzrz uzuz czcz mzmz ezez iziz xzxz ,z,z wzwz ozoz a.a. ;.;. s.s. l.l.

Apply the keys you know	The zealous amongst us are always whizzing from task to task. In Zone Z in Zurich, there are jazz concerts every Friday. I am not lazy although I tire easily.

Word groupings	fill, hill, drill, grill, skill, till, mill, bill. low, bow, cow, how, mow, now, row, sow, tow, wow, vow. constant, constraint, consent, contain, confess, cone.

Speed and accuracy	Aim to key in each drill in one minute with no more than two errors Mary would like to go to the theatre next week. We shall go with her. (14 words per minute)

Q Use the **A** finger

P Use the **;** finger

| **Tip** | Always proof read your work to see if you have made any errors. |

Review keys

asdf ;lkj ol,k tnie mkir vnbh yfjv zircon, zombie,
zebra, zest, ziggurat, zillion, zinc, zing, earthog,
orange, olive, Orlando, Oliver, Zara, Zak, zone, jazz

Practise new keys

qpqp pqpq qpqp pqpq qpqp pqqp qpqp pqpq qpqp pqpq qpqp
aqsq dqfq ;plp kpjp apsp dpfp ;qlq kqjq fqpa jpqk aqaq
;q;q sqsq lqlq dqdq kqkq fqfq jqjq gqgq hqhq tqtq yqtq
vqvq nqnq bqbq .q.q rqrq uquq cqcq mqmq eqeq iqiq xqxq
,q,q wqwq oqoq zqzq .q.q apap ;p;p spsp lplp dpdp kpkp
fpfp jpjp gpgp hphp tptp ypyp vpvp npnp bpbp .p.p rprp
upup cpcp mpmp epep ipip xpxp ,p,p wpwp opop zpzp .p.p

Apply the keys you know

Apparently, the only way to get there is by helicopter.
Quite amazing. The prerequisite is an NVQ in Business
Administration. Perhaps you could acquire it. Yes.

Word groupings

preview, precede, preempt, pretext, presume, predate.
old, bold, cold, fold, gold, hold, sold, told, boldly.

Speed and accuracy

Aim to key in each drill in one minute with no more than two errors

Deborah likes to go swimming each week. She says it
helps her to keep fit. 15 words per minute

! Use the **A** finger

? Use the **;** finger

: Use the **;** finger

Tip	Remember you will also need to use the shift key for the exclamation mark and question mark.

Review keys

judge, Witch, which, ordinary, whereabouts, Wise, wisdom, warthog, orange, olive, Orlando, with, what, would, when, will, gaga; jazz: zealous; task; Zone. concerts, wisdom, learn; bide: vandal, ghastly; abash.

Practise new keys

I love ice cream! Answer the following questions: Congratulations! What did you say? Help! Take note: What is your address? Attention! Look out! Why? Can I help you? Yes please! Please order the following: six pens, two notebooks and three staplers.

Apply the keys you know

When will she be arriving? How long will she be staying? Look over there! Help! Watch out! When is the train due to arrive? Listen! I have something important to tell you.

Word groupings

rising! leaving! moving! sailing! eating! swimming! ride? side? decide? abide? slide? wide? hide? ides? organise! realise? standardise! exorcise? exercise!

Speed and accuracy

Aim to key in each drill in one minute with no more than two errors

William is buying a black labrador puppy. He is going to call it Fido. It is six weeks old. <u>19 words per minute</u>

Browsing or surfing the Internet can be great fun. You can look at many different subjects this way. <u>20 words per minute</u>

Practise Paragraphs

Now you are familiar with the letters on the keyboard, try keying in some paragraphs. Remember to leave a clear line space between each by pressing the return key twice. Practise each paragraph twice aiming for complete accuracy each time.

Computers are being used more and more these days. Children are being taught information technology skills from a young age and many people now have computers in their homes. The use of electronic mail and the Internet has now become a very significant method of communication. <u>46 words, 56 'typing words'</u>

Dancing is a great way to keep fit. It provides aerobic exercise and is fun. Most towns will have a dance school that you can go to. Why not find a dancing partner and enrol in a class? There will be lots of classes to choose from including ballroom, tap and modern. <u>50 words, 54 'typing words'</u>

You can now key in all the letters of the alphabet. You will soon be able to build up quite a fast speed. Remember to keep keying at an even pace. You must leave a consistent number of spaces after a full stop. One or two spaces are acceptable. You should always leave a clear line space between paragraphs. <u>59 words, 62 'typing words'</u>

There are all sorts of unusual fruit and vegetables available in supermarkets these days. They tend to be quite expensive, but why not treat yourself once in a while and discover new tastes that you have never come across before? You will also be able to find cookery books that contain recipes for many of these strange and exotic foods. 60 words, 68 'typing words'

If you have trouble deciding which career would suit you, then you may find that your local Careers Office can help you. They can run a test on your experience, interests and skills and give you a list of possible careers. They will also be able to tell you if you need any further qualifications for the career that you decide upon. 62 words, 67 'typing words'

Word processing packages these days allow you to do so much more than just word process. Many of them allow you to draw various shapes, to insert images, or use colour to define your own documents. Are you using all of the functions of your word processing software? Why not try our series of books on different software packages and let us teach you new skills that will help you make the most of your word processing software?

77 words, 86 'typing words'

Do you find that you never have enough hours in the day? Do you have lots of things that you keep meaning to do but can never find enough time to do them? Why not book a time management consultation or try one of our time management courses? We will be able to teach you the skills that will help you organise your life more efficiently. You will be able to achieve much more each day and still have time for the things you like to do. 87 words, 88 'typing words'

Everybody needs a break sometimes. However, it is not always easy to find the money to take a holiday abroad. You need to pay for flights, accommodation, food and excursions amongst other things. If this is the case why not try a working holiday? Your accommodation and food will be paid for and you will still have time to visit the local area. You could work for a week and then with the money you have earned you could visit a bit more of the country. 86 words, 92 'typing words'

Do you have spare time on your hands? Have your children just started school? Perhaps you have recently retired? Why not come and try out some of our recreational courses? There are many different activities to choose from. If you are interested in cookery you could try our introductory and advanced courses in French and Italian cookery. Perhaps you would like to learn a new craft? You can choose from weaving, painting, calligraphy and pottery. We also have a number of language courses that are designed to give you a basic grounding in French, Italian, Spanish or German. After completing the course you will be able to go on holiday confident in the fact that you can ask for anything you need. <u>121 words, 141 'typing words'</u>

1 Use the **A** finger

2 Use the **S** finger

Tip	As well as the numbers located on the keyboard, there is usually an extra set of numbered keys to the right called a numeric keypad. If you prefer, you can use this keypad to key in numbers (see page 37).

Practise new keys

```
1221 1221 1212 2121 2112 2211 1212 2121 af12 ;j21 gh12

a1s2 d1f1 ;2l2 k2j1 a1s2 d1f1 ;2l2 k2j1 s12t 121d a12k

12kf 1ty2 1qw2 2m1n 1v2c 2gh2 w1k2 11r2 2s1j ;1a2 2b2m

z12x 2.1, 1d2e i1o2 2pu1 :2?1 !121 1?!2 1d21 e12i g1m2

2z1a f:21 !d?r uf22 2i2b v1,j 2gn1 2u2o 1212 ac12 22zp

12kf 1ty2 1qw2 2m1n 1v2c 2gh2 w1k2 11r2 2s1j ;1a2 2b2m
```

Apply the keys you know

There are 21 girls in the class. Over 122 entries were received. She cycled 21 miles today. The number of exam entries was 21. Over 12 people passed the exam. They were married on the 12th. My sister was 12 on Friday. I had a great party; 21 people came. The code for those is A1221. Can you order 12 packets please. If you multiply 11 by 11 you get 121. I am 21 years of age.

Word groupings

Best, jest, nest, pest, rest, test, vest, west, zest. Quad, quantity, quality, quip, quit, quill, quins.

Speed and accuracy drills

Aim to key in each drill in one minute with no more than two errors

Joseph keeps three white mice. They make excellent pets. They are called Victor, Queenie and Zena.

(20 words per minute)

| 8 | Use the **K** finger |
| 9 | Use the **L** finger |

Tip | Always check numbers carefully after keying them in.

Practise new keys

```
8998  8998  8989  9898  9889  9988  8989  9898  8998  8989  9889
a8s9  d9f9  ;9l9  k9j8  a8s9  d8f8  ;9l9  k9j8  s89k  l98d  a8s9
89kf  8ty9  8qw9  9m8n  8v9c  9gh9  w8k9  l8r9  9s8j  ;8a9  9b9m
z89x  9.8,  8d9e  i8o9  9pu8  :9?8  !898  8?!9  8d98  e89i  g8m9
9z8a  f:98  !d?r  uf99  9i9b  v8,j  9gn8  9u9o  8989  ac89  99zp
8998  8998  8989  9898  9889  9988  8989  9898  af89  ;j98  gh39
89kf  8ty9  8qw9  9m8n  8v9c  9gh9  w8k9  l8r9  9s8j  ;8a9  9b9m
```

Apply the keys you know

If you need an ambulance, then you should phone 999; in America you should phone 911. If you want to find out a telephone number you can try calling directory enquiries; their number is 192. I started my first full time job at the age of 19. I live at 912 San Francisco Boulevard. There were 219 people at the wedding reception. The zoo owned 19 snakes 9 monkeys, 12 penguins and 2 lions.

Word groupings

age, sage, savage, enrage, pillage, cage, stage, wage delirious, serious, cautious, spacious, hilarious

Speed and accuracy

Aim to key in this drill in one minute with no more than two errors

Lucy enjoys swimming and wishes to join a swimming club. This would enable her to compete in galas.

29 words a minute

3 Use the **D** finger

4 Use the **F** finger

| Tip | If you are keying in a post code leave one clear space between the two parts – e.g. N22 7PJ. If you are keying in decimal numbers use the full stop as the decimal point – e.g. 0.34. |

Practise new keys	4434 4334 1414 2424 3434 4444 3434 4444 8484 9494 1313
	a3s4 d3f3 ;414 k4j3 a3s4 d4f4 ;313 k4j3 s34k 143d a3s4
	2323 3333 4343 4343 8383 9393 0303 1414 2424 3434 4444
	8484 9494 0404 i93m 12nk 98as df34 43tg c3b4 b34v x3z3
	4.1. 2,4n 39xj d19i 4n3v 434y 4gh3 !43. a93b 484z 48op
	3h9o p84w 3u4p ,2.8 3p4q r81v 9i3o a1;3 3n4i 98k4 2o3q

Apply the keys you know

The date of the meeting is 24 April. Over 340 people attended the conference. There are 43 houses in the street. Susan was born on the 14th of May. Their wedding anniversary is the 31st of January. My father was born in 1934 and my mother was born in 1939. There were 934 people on board the liner. Please order 9 boxes of folders: code Z8349; 3 boxes of envelopes: code P9214 and 4 boxes of pens: code H1469. I would like 3 teaspoons of sugar, please. Please make 24 copies of the report for me.

Word groupings

Come, dome, gnome, some, omega, omen, omelette, Rome.

Speed and accuracy

Aim to key in this drill in one minute with no more than two errors

The office administrator has a very responsible job. She must ensure that everything runs smoothly.

(20 words per minute)

6 Use the **J** finger

7 Use the **J** finger

Tip Twelve-hour clock times are keyed as 9.00pm – use a full stop between the figures. Twenty-four-hour clock times are keyed as 0900 hrs, 2330 hrs, etc – no full stop is required.
Be consistent when keyboarding times and figures, your work will look much better.

Practise new keys

```
7767  7667  1717  2727  6767  7777  6767  7777  8787  9797  1616

a6s7  d6f6  ;717  k7j6  a6s7  d7f7  ;616  k7j6  s6fk  176d  a6s7

2626  6666  7676  7676  8686  9696  0606  1717  2727  6767  7777

8787  9797  0707  i96m  12nk  98as  df67  76tg  c6b7  b67v  x6z6

7.1.  2,7n  69xj  d19i  7n6v  767y  7gh6  !76.  a96b  787z  78op

6h9o  p87w  6u7p  ,2.8  6p7q  r81v  9i6o  a1;6  6n7i  98k7  2o6q
```

Apply the keys you know

The school has 1167 students and 73 teachers. The cake needs to be cut into 17 segments. We have travelled 712 miles in less than 3 days. The odds are 17 to 1. The order has arrived but there are only 19 boxes of biros, not 26 as we ordered. I have booked a holiday for 7 days in Austria.

Word groupings

Numb, thumb, lumber, Rhumba, dumber, plumb, number

Speed and accuracy

Aim to key in this drill in one minute with no more than two errors

Please type a report from my handwritten draft. Please proof read it carefully before returning it.

(20 words per minute)

5 Use the **F** finger

0 Use the **;** finger

| Tip | Use the tab key to line up your numbered lists. Find out how to set tabs on your software now. |

Practice new keys	5050	1525	3040	7585	1059	8057
	6512	0851	7502	3504	6100	5508
	3051	6805	5500	1056	2507	8509

Apply the keys you know

1   Over 600 people bought a mobile phone this week.

2   I am going on holiday in 10 days.

3   Lucy received 25 birthday cards this year.

4   Margaret is hosting a party for 150 people.

5   Please arrange for 250,000 catalogues to be printed.

6   You need to organise catering for 900 people and accommodation for 550.

7   When you go to the shops, could you pick up 10 loaves of bread?

8   We will be interviewing 10 people and then we will select 2 people for second interviews.

9   More than 50 people were invited, but only 20 turned up.

10 You should cook the meat for 25 minutes per 500g plus an extra 25 minutes at gas mark 5.

Word groupings

Cup, pup, sup, upper, upward, update, upgrade, uphill.

"₂ Use the **S** finger   **&₇** Use the **J** finger

£₃ Use the **D** finger   ***₈** Use the **K** finger

$₄ Use the **F** finger   **(₉** Use the **L** finger

^₅ Use the **J** finger   **)₀** Use the **;** finger

> The location of the symbol keys may vary from keyboard to keyboard. However, if a symbol appears in a different position on your keyboard, find the correct home key finger and press the required key.
>
> The symbols shown above the numbers can be keyed by holding down the shift key and keying in the relevant number. Remember to use the shift key (not the caps lock key) when keying in symbols shown on the upper half of a key.

Apply the keys you know

1   Jane (my cousin) will visit us soon.

2   The handbag cost £45.00.

3   The cost of the flight to America is $300.

4   The name of the solicitor is Hayes & Wise Ltd.

5   Sale! All clothes reduced!

6   "Watch out!" he shouted, "the ice is broken".

7   Over 50% of the houses in the street have garages.

8   The clothes can be delivered in 3 days (UK only).

9   Use the ^ caret symbol or the * asterix as
      wildcards when running a database query.

10   Jones & Son gave the most competitive quote.

 Use the ; finger   **Use the ; finger**

 Use the ; finger   **Use the ; finger**

| Tip | Remember to use the shift key when keying in symbols shown on the upper half of a key. |

Apply the keys you know

1   The line key is used for a horizontal line _____

2   Buy now — pay later.

3   Part-time vacancies are popular with working
    mothers.

4   318 + 5172 = 5490

5   £2.38 + £5.59 = £7.97

6   Do you know how much a rail ticket will cost from
    London to Manchester?

7   My web-site address is http://www.keyboarding.html.
    What's yours?

8   You can buy a pack of ten workbooks @ £10 each for
    only £90.

9   How many times a week do you go swimming?

10 It's only $40 which is quite a bargain.

11 My e-mail address is J_Smith@server.com.

12 The reference quoted is 624/93/SL/DP.

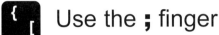 Use the **;** finger   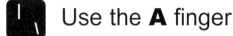 Use the **A** finger

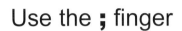 Use the **;** finger   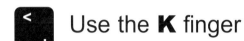 Use the **K** finger

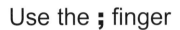 Use the **;** finger   Use the **L** finger

Tip	These are the remaining symbols on the keyboard. Ensure you know where these keys are and don't forget the shift key must be used when typing symbols shown on the upper half of a key – even when the caps lock is on.

Apply the keys you know

1   If you have a common name you may need to add symbols to it to create an e-mail address that hasn't already been assigned. For example John~Smith@server.com or Fred_Brown@server.com.

2   [Please remember to insert the figures] {10+35.5+25}.

3   My library code is 90##2229##2.

4   If you want to search for people who joined the club in or before 1995, then you need to key in: <=1995.

5   The Spanish use a ~ (tilda) on the letter n to change the sound [ny].

6   You have been sent a virtual card – go to http://www.cards.com and key in this code: 931#\\00123+\\#11213 to see your card.

Speed and accuracy

Aim to key in each drill in one minute with no more than two errors

Quentin is a lazy student. He must study much harder if he is to excel in any of his exam subjects. (20 words per minute)

A receptionist's duties are many and varied. However the most important part of the job is to be able to communicate well with others. (27 words per minute)

The beautiful colours of the autumn leaves can be seen everywhere. Long brisk walks in the park or countryside will give great pleasure to all. (29 words per minute)

If your duties include opening the post every day it is important that you do this efficiently. Any items that are marked 'urgent' should be dealt with first. (32 words per minute)

Judith always finishes her work as quickly as possible so that she can go home early. Sometimes she does not check her work carefully and it is full of errors. (32 words per minute)

Selecting a perfume is a very personal thing to do. Only try one or two at a time. Allow a few minutes for the perfume to settle on your skin before making a final decision. (35 words per minute)

Knitting and sewing are skills that are dying out today. This is because people do not have the time to learn them. The materials are also expensive and it is often cheaper to buy items rather than make them. (42 words per minute or 21 words per minute – 2 minute timing)

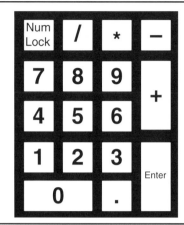

| Tip | When using the numeric keypad, use the left thumb to key in spaces. |

As well as the numbers located on the keyboard, there is usually an extra set of numbered keys to the right called a numeric keypad. This pad also has an enter key which has the same use as the return or enter key on the main keyboard.

To use these keys you need to make sure the number lock is on – on some computers it will automatically be turned on when you start and on others it will be turned off. To turn it on, press the number lock key at the top left-hand corner of the keypad.

Use your right hand to key in figures on the numeric keypad.

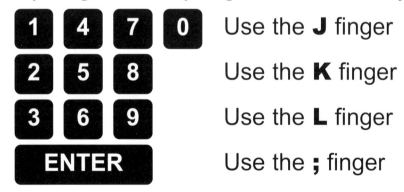

1 4 7 0   Use the **J** finger

2 5 8   Use the **K** finger

3 6 9   Use the **L** finger

ENTER   Use the **;** finger

The keypad also has mathematical symbols which can be used in computing.

/ Use the **K** finger   – Use the **;** finger

* Use the **L** finger   + Use the **;** finger

Abbreviations

If you are taking a keyboarding exam, then read this section carefully, otherwise move onto the next section.

When you are keying in from draft, you will often find that abbreviations have been used. This applies to the workplace as well as in examinations. As a keyboard operator you will need to know:

- what the abbreviations stand for
- how to spell the word in full.

Listed below are the abbreviations you can expect to come across. All the abbreviations are shown using open punctuation.

info	information	ref(s)	reference
necy	necessary	ref(d)	refer or referred
opp(s)	opportunity or opportunities	sec(s)	secretary or secretaries
org	organisation	yr(s)	year(s)
poss	possible	yr(s)	your(s)

You will see from the list that some abbreviations have two or more meanings. This means that you will have to read the draft carefully to find out which word to use. Be particularly careful with refer and reference; year and your.

As well as the abbreviations given above, you must also remember to write the following words in full.

- Days of the week
- Months of the year
- Words in addresses – for example, road for *rd*; street for *st*, etc.
- Complimentary Close – for example, Yours faithfully for *Yrs ffly*; Yours sincerely for *Yrs sncly*

Try keying in the following sentences, showing the abbreviations in full and spelling them correctly.

1   The info given to the sec was confidential.
2   How many secs are employed by yr org?
3   Will it be poss for us to meet later this yr?
4   It will be necy to take up refs for the new member
     of staff.
5   We must act quickly or the opp will be lost.
6   I ref to yr recent letter received on Weds.
7   In Feb we will move to Oaklands Cres.
8   The new spring launch will take place in Apr.
9   Carole's address is 75 Queen Sq, Leicester.
10   I hope to receive the necy info by the first week
     of Jan.
11   It will not be poss to give you the necy info
     today.
12   The sec refd to the senior manager before giving
     out the info.
13   The org has a policy to hold a pay review each yr.
14   Yr ref was excellent.
15   There are many opps for secs today.

Now key in the following paragraph, expanding all the abbreviations.

There are many opps for trained secs in the business
world today. It is necy to make yourself look
presentable when attending interview. If you don't, it
is poss that this may lower yr chances. Make sure you
include on your curriculum vitae how many yrs
experience you have. Don't forget to tell your referees
that they may be asked for refs. Find out a bit about
the org you are applying to before you attend the
interview.

Spelling

The words that have been underlined in the following sentences are often incorrectly spelt. Key in the sentences and then check your work carefully, paying particular attention to the highlighted words.

1   In the <u>absence</u> of instruction, I have <u>decided</u> to <u>complete</u> the <u>correspondence</u> myself.

2   I would <u>appreciate</u> some <u>assistance</u> in finding <u>suitable</u> <u>accommodation</u>.

3   The <u>European</u> <u>financial</u> markets were performing well in <u>January</u>.

4   To avoid <u>disappointment</u>, please check the catalogue description <u>carefully</u>.

5   In order to become a <u>solicitor</u>, Michael had to pass a number of <u>professional</u> qualifications.

6   I know it is <u>inconvenient</u>, but please make this work your first <u>priority</u>.

7   The <u>miniature</u> <u>ceramic</u> vases are <u>irreplaceable</u>.

8   I <u>sincerely</u> hope you will <u>succeed</u> in your <u>chosen</u> <u>career</u>.

9   The <u>campaign</u> to recruit <u>volunteers</u> to work for the charity was <u>successful</u>.

10 The <u>facilities</u> at the <u>conference</u> <u>centre</u> are <u>exceptional</u>.

11 The <u>references</u> provided by Elizabeth were <u>satisfactory</u>.

12 Thank you for your recent <u>enquiry</u> regarding the <u>purchase</u> of three new <u>computers</u>.

13 It was with great <u>enthusiasm</u> that the <u>committee</u> <u>appointed</u> John as the managing <u>director</u>.

14 I would like you to <u>install</u> a new kitchen in my
    <u>extension</u>.

15 You must repay your <u>mortgage</u> in monthly
    <u>instalments</u>.

16 The <u>guarantee</u> for our <u>manufacturing</u> <u>equipment</u> runs
    out in <u>February</u>.

17 I have <u>received</u> your <u>documents</u> <u>referring</u> to the new
    <u>premises</u>.

18 The <u>administrator</u> was given a three month <u>temporary</u>
    contract.

19 I would be <u>extremely</u> <u>grateful</u> if you could
    <u>acknowledge</u> <u>receipt</u> of this letter.

20 In my <u>experience</u> the <u>auditors</u> are rarely
    <u>inaccurate</u>.

Now key in the following sentences correcting any spelling errors.

1   The catelogue was a huge dissapointment

2   The monthly installments on the morgage were
    extremelly high.

3   The commitee dicided to make finding suitible
    premeses a prioriety.

4   The advertising champaign should suceed.

5   In Janury, we shall be attending a confrence.

6   It is inconvenent, but I am sure we will be able to
    do it.

7   The financal direcler was refering to the Europaen
    markets.

8   Corespondence was checked carefuly by a soliciter.

9   At the sports center you will be able to use the
    squash courts.

10 Please compleat the enqury form.

Homophones

Homophones are words that sound similar but have different meanings. Make sure that you always use the correct word.

In the following examples, the correct word has been underlined. Key in the following sentences and then check your work carefully.

1   The <u>principal</u>/principle told the students that they must purchase their own stationary/<u>stationery</u>.

2   I would advice/<u>advise</u> you to take the <u>advice</u>/advise of a solicitor in this matter.

3   You should <u>accept</u>/except the complement/<u>compliment</u> graciously.

4   It will be grate/<u>great</u> to see you again next weak/<u>week</u>.

5   Please prepare a draught/<u>draft</u> document for the committee.

6   The letter was <u>personal</u>/personnel.

7   I am pleased to say I have <u>passed</u>/past all my examinations.

8   Lesley should cheque/<u>check</u> the letters before they are sent.

9   You should right/<u>write</u> to Judith and <u>formally</u>/formerly <u>accept</u>/except her invitation.

10 It is plane/<u>plain</u> to <u>see</u>/sea that the <u>current</u>/currant situation is not good.

Now key in the following sentences, choosing the correct word from the ones in square brackets. If you are unsure of any of the words then look them up in a dictionary.

1   Jason read the passage [allowed/aloud].

2   The [source/sauce] of the news item was not known.

3   Hurry up. It is [all ready/already] late.

4   The mouse's [tale/tail] was rather long.

5   I [here/hear] [ewe/you] are a [great/grate]
    sportswoman.

6   The curtains certainly [complemented/complimented]
    the carpet.

7   I will [waive/wave] the fee on this occasion.

8   The [bored/board] of directors was appointed some
    time ago.

9   Do not forget to [practice/practise] your guitar
    every day.

10 I do not know [whether/weather] they will be able
    to attend.

11 Please [right/write] a letter to Mrs Jones.

12 [Witch/Which] direction should we take?

13 You have had [too/to] many days [of/off] recently.

14 There are [so/sew] many things to do.

15 I would like you to [meat/meet] the
    [principle/principal].

Double Letters

It can sometimes be difficult to key in words that contain double letters – sometimes you end up keying three of the same letter, and sometimes only one.

Key in the following sentences and then check your work carefully to make sure you have keyed in all the double letters correctly.

1   Betty called for her mummy and daddy.

2   Julia was married on a hot, sunny day.

3   Swimming is a good exercise for people of all ages.

4   The letter from the committee should arrive tomorrow.

5   I guarantee you will enjoy the programme.

6   Unfortunately we are committed to providing this service.

7   It will not be possible to take up this opportunity at the current time.

8   Occasionally, we have supper with business colleagues.

9   I will need to recruit additional employees if the job is to be completed.

10 Samuel's occupation takes him abroad occasionally.

Displaying Text

Now you have learnt the keyboard, you can start to display text in different ways

Text Alignment

Text alignment refers to the way in which text is set out on the page. There are four main types of text alignment. Try keyboarding the different examples below.

> This text is called **left** aligned. This means that each line of text starts in the same place at the left hand margin, giving a neat line down the page. The text ends in different places at the right-hand margin – this is known as a ragged right margin. This is the best alignment for letters.

> This text is called **right** aligned. This means that the text is aligned from the right-hand margin, leaving a ragged left-hand margin. This is only used for display purposes.

> This text is called **centre** aligned. This means that each line is centred from the middle of the typing line. The 'typing line' is the space that is left between the margins – in other words the area in which you keyboard.
> This alignment should only be used for display purposes.

> This text is called **justified**. This means that the text starts and ends at each margin. In order to do this, the word processing software may add extra space between words. This alignment is useful if you are keying in reports or newsletters.

Whichever alignment you choose, make sure you are consistent throughout a document, your work will look much better.

Headings   When displaying work, you may want to use a main heading and/or a sub-heading for emphasis. Main headings are displayed at the top of a document and usually have the most emphasis. Sub-headings come after a main heading and are not as prominent. When designing work, remember that a simple, clear, easy-to-read approach is best. Try to keep your headings in the same style or typeface – changing the typesize and/or emboldening is often all that is needed. To add emphasis you can use bold, centre, underline, or italics. You can also use block capitals (all capitals), spaced capitals or initial capitals (a capital letter to start each word), though initial capitals may not be suitable if you have sub-headings in the document.

Try keying in the examples below:

MAIN HEADING – BLOCKED CAPITALS AND BOLD (14pt font)

Sub-heading – initial capitals and bold (12pt font)

<u>Main Heading – Bold And Underline Emphasis</u> (12pt font)

Subheading – italics and bold (12 pt font)

<u>MAIN HEADING – BLOCKED CAPITALS, CENTRED
AND UNDERLINED EMPHASIS</u>

Sub-heading – initial capitals and centred

Note that whichever style has been used, there is a clear line space between the main heading and the text.

Documents

The documents which follow will provide you with the opportunity to practise your keyboarding and layout skills.

You do not need to press return at the end of each line – the text will flow from line to line automatically. Depending on the font and font size you are using, you will not necessarily fit the same number of words on a line as shown in the exercises which follow. This is because each font has its own sizing and each letter is a different width (see page 5). Experiment with fonts and sizes to find one you like. Try and use different size fonts to emphasise headings.

When printing out the business documents, use Print Preview to decide how many spaces to leave at the top of the page and/or in between sections and/or paragraphs to ensure a neat appearance.

There are six each of the following documents for you to keyboard:

- articles
- personal business letters
- memos
- notices for display

Some of the drafts are keyed in and some are handwritten. It is important that you start to practise keying in from handwritten draft as this is the most common form of draft in the workplace.

Articles and Reports

You may be asked to write a report or article for a research project in school, college or in the workplace.

These are generally presented as longer paragraphs of text with a main heading.

- Experiment with different styles of heading to give them more or less emphasis.

- Experiment with different line spacing for the paragraphs of text, although remember that it will look better if you are consistent within a document.

- Once you have finished keying in the piece, check your document to ensure you have not made any errors.

Now you have completed the keyboard, you should be able to complete each one in under 20 minutes. Try keying in the articles/reports which follow.

Article 1 Key in the following article as shown.

The Lewis Animal Sanctuary

The Lewis Animal Sanctuary is privately run and depends entirely upon donations. We care for all types of animal and we never turn away an unwanted or mistreated animal no matter how little room we have.

Much of our work concerns pets such as dogs and cats. However, at present we are also caring for 2 ponies, 14 ducks and 3 badgers. We rely on help from volunteers to look after the animals. We enjoy an excellent working relationship with a national charity.

All our funding comes from public donation. If you would like to donate a sum of money you will be helping us to provide these animals with a better life.

If you would like to become one of our volunteers and can spare a few hours each week, please contact us. We would be delighted to hear from you.

Aim for completion in **15** minutes.

Article 2   Key in the following article as shown.

DIGITAL TELEVISION

In 1998, digital television was introduced in the UK. Subscribers to this service can now have access to a large number of television channels.

There are three ways to have digital television installed in your home. You can have a satellite dish fitted, buy a box which is linked through your telephone line, or purchase a digital television set.

The satellite option will also allow you access, provided you subscribe, to satellite television such as Sky. If you already own a satellite dish it may need to be adjusted. The box option means that you have a box, the size of a small video recorder connected to your television set and to a telephone line. At present the number of channels obtained through this method is limited, although it is anticipated that this will increase shortly. If you purchase a digital television then you will not need a box or a satellite dish.

As well as ensuring you have the correct equipment you will also need to subscribe to a digital television provider. Costs vary depending on the number of channels to which you have access. However, at present it is in the region of £10–£30 per month.

Aim for completion in **20 minutes.**

Article 3   Key in the following article as shown.

NVQ Qualifications

National Vocational Qualifications, or NVQ's were designed to help people in the workplace obtain qualifications that relate to their work. They were also designed so that people could be awarded a qualification that recognises the work they are already doing.

For example, if you work as a sales assistant in the retail trade you may be able to use your experience and training to prove your competency in the workplace and at your job. This may lead to being awarded an NVQ qualification. Your competency can be assessed in a variety of ways including observation, questionning and a portfolio of 'evidence'.

There are many different NVQ qualifications covering many different careers. Why not find out if your organisation has a training scheme that will allow you to obtain one of these qualifications?

Key in the following article as shown.

TOURING HOLIDAYS

Coach tours can be a relaxing way to spend your holiday. You may enjoy seeing a number of towns and cities without having to do any of the driving. Modern coaches are extremely comfortable and have all amenities including a drinks machine.

You can book a touring holiday to one of any number of destinations in this country and in Europe. One of the most popular trips is a weekend in Paris. Our company offers an excellent weekend break to Paris. Prices include accommodation at a three-star hotel. All hotel rooms have private en-suite facilities.

If you would like further information or a brochure, please contact our reservations staff. They will be delighted to help you.

Aim for completion in **10** minutes.

Article 5   Key in the following article as shown.

Designing a kitchen

If you are planning a new kitchen there are many points to consider. The size of your kitchen obviously needs to be taken into account. However, you will also need to be clear about how your kitchen will be used.

For example, if you are going to use the kitchen as a dining area then this may affect the layout of the units and cooker etc.

Another consideration is the number of appliances you need to have in your room. If you do not have a separate utility room then you may need to make space for a washing machine and tumble dryer. If you add in a cooker, diswasher, fridge, freezer and microwave oven there may not be much room for cupboards.

The use of a specialist kitchen designer can be invaluable in helping you design the most effective and efficient layout. They will often provide detailed plans for a small fee. Your local telephone directory will give you contact numbers for kitchen designers.

Aim for completion in **15** minutes.

Article 6   Key in the following article as shown.

Tropical Leisure Centre

The Tropical Leisure Centre is one of the most up-to-date centres in this country. It boasts a large indoor pool and a heated outdoor pool.

There is a skating rink, ten-pin bowling alley and games room, so that the whole family can enjoy a day out. Meals and refreshments can be obtained from our tropical themed restaurant.

Parties are our speciality. You can hold your child's birthday party at the centre from just £7.00 per child, including food. The centre can also be hired during the evenings for larger parties and company outings.

The centre is open from 7.30 am until 11 pm, 7 days per week. For further information including prices, please contact our main reception desk on 01839 37573.

Aim for completion in **10** minutes.

Personal Letters

A personal letter is a formal letter usually sent by an individual rather than a company. You may need to send a letter requesting information on a company to help you complete a project for school or college. Use Print Preview to help you decide on the exact number of spaces to leave between items.

Stationery

You should use plain A4 paper.

Style

Blocked style is the most popular style for a letter. Everything starts at the left-hand margin including the paragraphs. Leave at least one clear line space between items.

Margins

Use the default (see page 5) or 2.5 cm at top, bottom, left and right.

Point size

Point size 10 or 12 is suitable for letters.

Name and address

With personal letters the address of the person sending the letter is keyed in first. This takes the place of headed notepaper that would generally be used if you were writing a letter on behalf of a company or business. There is no need to emphasise the address block and all lines should be keyed in at the left-hand margin.

Punctuation

Open punctuation is widely used in letters. This means that the only parts of the letter to have punctuation are the paragraphs of text.

Date

All letters should include the current date. Leave a clear line space after your name and address and type the date in full, including the year. If using open punctuation do not type in 'th, nd, st or rd'.

Complimentary close

The complimentary close consists of Yours sincerely or Yours faithfully – the first if you know the person's name and the second if you don't.

Continuation pages

Whenever your work goes on to a second page, you must remember to number it. Use plain paper and number this page at the top. There is no need to key in the date and the name of the addressee at the top of the page.

Signature block

The signature block gives space for the person writing the letter to sign his/her name. It is usual to leave five clear spaces after the complimentary close to make space for the signature and then the name is keyed in underneath.

Enclosures

If you are enclosing something with a letter, for example a cheque or a copy of a document, then it should be indicated at the bottom of the letter. Leave one clear space after the name and complimentary close and then key in Enc.

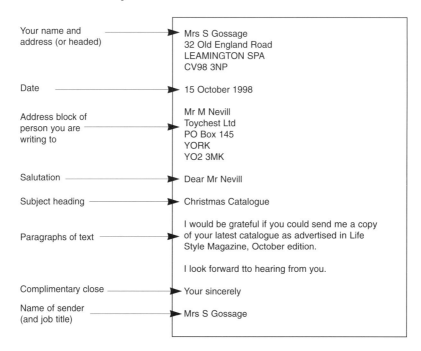

You should be able to complete each letter in approximately 20 minutes

Letter 1   Key in the following letter as shown.

48 Milton Ave
LAUNCESTON
Cornwall
LN3 2WQ

(today's date)

Lewis Animal Sanctuary
Briar Lane
LAUNCESTON
Cornwall
LN27 3PE

Dear Sir

I have recently become aware of the work you do with abandoned animals through your information leaflet. I am sending you a cheque for £50 as a donation for the Sanctuary.

Your leaflet states that you require volunteers to help care for the animals. I believe that I could help on a regular basis of 2 or 3 hours per week. Although I have not had any experience of working with animals I have been a pet owner - 2 dogs, 3 cats for a number of years.

If you feel I could be of any assistance, please contact me.

Yours faithfully

Georgia Reed

Aim for completion in **20** minutes.

Letter 2   Key in the following letter as shown.

3 Walcot Road
CARLISLE
CA62 9SP

(today's date)

Allen & King
45 Conway Road
CARLISLE
CA59 3NW

Dear Sirs

I read with interest your advertisement in the local
newspaper regarding digital television. I am interested in
having this service installed in my home.

At present I subscribe to a cable television network. Would it
be possible for me to keep the cable network as well as
having digital television? How would this work? I am
assuming that I would not need a satellite dish or a box as it
could be tuned through the cable network. Is this correct?

I would be grateful if you could telephone me on 01382
471920 to arrange for a 'free consultation' as stated in your
advertisement.

I look forward to meeting you.

Yours faithfully

Philip Challenger

Aim for completion in **20** minutes.

Letter 3

Key in the following letter as shown.

62 Barrow Road
Saltford
BRISTOL
BS1   4KZ

(today's date)

Ms   L   Shellard
Course Tutor
St Andrew's College
BATH
BA17 9DP

Dear Ms Shellard

Please find enclosed a completed enrolment form together with a cheque for £175. As you will see, I wish to enrol on the Business Administration NVQ Level 3 course, reference number 321A.

I note that the information given in the prospectus states that in order to enrol you should have the necessary relevant experience or qualifications. I have recently completed an NVQ Level 2 and have been working as a personal secretary for over 4 years.

The prospectus states that the first class will be held on 28 September at 7.00pm.   I look forward to meeting you.

Yours sincerely

Iris Banks

Enc

Aim for completion in **20 minutes**.

Letter 4   Key in the following letter as shown.

62 Arundel Rd
PRESTON
Lancs
PR22 9XL

(today's date)

Mr V Eccles
Bright Holidays plc
3B Johnson Street
PRESTON
Lancs
PR4 8QT

Dear Mr Eccles

I would be grateful if you could send me details of your coach tours as advertised in this week's local paper. I am particularly interested in a holiday in Italy.

My sister will be my travelling companion. We will require twin-bedroomed accommodation at all hotels. En-suite facilities are essential. Please advise me if this is standard on your tours.

I would welcome your early reply.

Yours sincerely

Mrs P Langdon

Aim for completion in **15** minutes.

Letter 5   Key in the following letter as shown.

14 The Beeches
LANCASTER
LA6 5DV

(today's date)

Countryside Kitchens
28 Hamilton Street
LANCASTER
LA6 7SM

Dear Sirs

Your company has been recommended to me by a friend. I am interested in having my kitchen re-fitted. I would be pleased if you would quote for this work.

My current kitchen units all need replacing and I am considering the purchase of new appliances. The room also needs new flooring and re-decoration.

Please telephone me to arrange an appointment. I can be contacted during working hours on 0161 321954. I have a copy of your current brochure. The Cotswold range of units would be the most suitable for my home.

I look forward to hearing from you.

Yours faithfully

Mrs B Latham

Aim for completion in **15** minutes.

Letter 6   Key in the following letter as shown.

122 Sharpe's Cres
CHARMOUTH
Devon
CH2 3NI

(today's date)

Ms Joyce Hill
Tropical Leisure Centre
CHARMOUTH
Devon
CH5 9OX

Dear Ms Hill

I read with interest your advertisement for a Deputy Manager at the
Tropical Leisure Centre. I would like you to consider my application
for this vacancy.

My previous experience in this area is considerable. I worked as a
Deputy Manager at the Oasis Leisure Centre in Bristol for three
years. This was a very interesting and rewarding position. I had to
leave this position in order to move to this area of the country.

A copy of my Curriculum Vitae is attached for your information.
References can be supplied on request.

I look forward to hearing from you.

Yours sincerely

Robert Allen

Enc

Aim for completion in **20** minutes.

Memos

A memorandum or memo is a document used to send messages to colleagues within an organisation. Memos can be formal documents or informal notes. You can use pre-printed paper or a template on the computer. Use the tab key to line up the entries you are keying in. One of the main differences between letters and memos is that memos do not have a signature block

Try keyboarding the example memo below. Leave one clear line space between items including after the last pre-printed entry.

Memorandum

To   Mark Dale

From Lisa Vane

Ref   MD/LV/1829

Date 29 November ——

I have received several complaints regarding the set of mixing bowls that are featured in the new catalogue. Apparently the packaging used has been insufficient and a number of bowls have been broken in transit.

Could you please look into this matter and report back to me within the next week.

Experiment with different heading styles for the subject heading.

Now you have completed the keyboard, you should be able to key in each memo in under 15 minutes.

Memo 1   Key in the following memo as shown.

MEMORANDUM

To   Lucy Watson

From   Jacob King

Ref   OP/JK

Date   (today's date)

OPEN DAY

I hope that the preparations for the open day are going smoothly. As you know there are only three weeks to go before the day itself.

Janice tells me that the notices for the event have been distributed around the town. She also says that it is possible the local newspaper is going to feature the Sanctuary two days before the event so that we can have some free publicity.

I believe that we have sufficient volunteers to help with the event. Perhaps you would be kind enough to check that this is the case and let me know if we require any more.

Aim for completion in **10** minutes

Key in the following memo as shown.

MEMORANDUM

To   Nick Coombs

From   George Hughes

Ref   GH/NC

Date   (today's date)

Digital Television Advertisement

As you know, a full-page advertisement was placed in the local newspaper last week. I am pleased to say it has been an outstanding success with over 500 enquiries. I believe that as we offered a free consultation, people are keen to take advantage of this.

The problem we now have is that we do not have enough trained staff to meet the demands of the response. I feel we shall have to do some training immediately so that we can send our staff out to conduct the free consultations.

I will prepare some training materials, including a sheet that the staff can take with them on their calls, today. Would you please check the materials later today before they are given to the staff? If you feel they are suitable then we can hold a training session first thing tomorrow morning.

At present Steven is arranging appointments with customers who telephone asking for a consultation. The postal enquiries are being left for a few days until we have more staff to deal with them.

Aim for completion in **10** minutes

Memo 3   Key in the following memo as shown.

MEMORANDUM

To   Francine Carter

From   Alison Lunt

Ref   HCT/129

Date   (today's date)

European Coach Tours

The advertising campaign for our European coach tours has been very successful. The response rate was high with approximately 50% of enquiries converting into firm bookings.

In view of this success I feel we should extend the campaign to include our coach tours in America. Bookings for these holidays have not been as high as expected this year. It may be that the advertising will provide us with the opportunity to increase these bookings.

I am sending you some information regarding suitable advertising for you to look at.

Aim for completion in **10** minutes.

Memo 4   Key in the following memo as shown.

MEMORANDUM

To   Jacob King

From   Lucy Shellard

Ref   LS/NVQ/1

Date   (today's date)

We have now received over 600 enrolment forms for NVQ in Business Administration Course. As you will appreciate, this is too many for one class. I have looked through the enrolment forms and the numbers are evenly spread between levels 2, 3 and 4.

I suggest that we split the group into 3 separate levels. I have spoken to the teaching staff and they are willing to take on the extra classes. I would be pleased to have your comments.

Aim for completion in **10** minutes.

Memo 5 Key in the following memo as shown.

MEMORANDUM

To   Joyce Hill

From   Peter Mitchell

Ref   DP/TLC

Date   (today's date)

DEPUTY MANAGER POSITION

The advertisement for the position of Deputy Manager appeared in the local newspaper today. I hope that we will receive a good response to this advertisement.

The closing date for applications is 28 July. We will then need to draw up a short list of applicants to interview. If possible may I suggest the following Monday afternoon for this. If all goes well, we should interview 6 applicants for this position. We can agree a date for the interviews later on.

Aim for completion in **10** minutes.

Memo 6

Key in the following memo as shown.

Memorandum

To   Mark Walsh

From   Petra Davies

Ref   PD/mw

Date   (today's date)

I have received a letter from a Mrs Latham. She is interested in having her kitchen re-fitted. The letter states that new appliances, flooring and re-decoration will also be required.

Please call Mrs Latham to arrange an appointment to discuss her requirements in detail. She can be contacted on 0161 321954. I would be grateful if you could do this as soon as possible. It may be necessary for you to take Paul with you.

For your information, Mrs Latham feels that the Cotswold range of units would be the most suitable.

Aim for completion in **10 minutes**.

NOTICES FOR DISPLAY

You may want to produce a notice for display purposes at school, college, the workplace or in your social life. These should be eye-catching and interesting to read. In order to make a notice easy to read the line endings should be short and there should be plenty of space throughout the document.

Experiment with different fonts and font sizes to make your notice more attractive. Do not use too many fonts, though, as this will look cluttered.

Items in lists should be displayed on separate lines rather than all on the same line as this will look more eye catching.

Now you have completed the keyboard, you should be able to key in each notice in under 10 minutes.

Notice 1   Key in the following notice as shown.

<u>Lewis Animal Sanctuary</u>

The Lewis Animal Sanctuary is holding an Open Day on 24 July.

Come along and see the work we do.

We help care for animals that have been abandoned or mistreated.

The Open Day is a day out for the whole family.

Attractions include:

Raffle
Games
Competitions
Animal show

We look forward to seeing you.

Aim for completion in **10** minutes

Notice 2   Key in the following notice as shown.

DIGITAL TELEVISION

Would you like to subscribe to digital television, but do not know how to go about it?

Do you need to purchase a satellite dish or a 'box'?

What happens if you already subscribe to satellite or cable television?

Is a new television necessary in order to have digital television?

Allen & King are experts in installing digital television. Why not let them give you a free consultation, in your own home, to assess the best method of digital television for you?

Call 01382 293810 now to arrange an appointment.

Aim for completion in **15** minutes

Notice 3   Key in the following notice and add emphasis.

Business Administration

Are you currently working in an office?

Would you like to gain a qualification
in Business Administration?

Why not enrol on one of our courses
which leads to a recognised qualification?

We offer courses at

Level One
Level Two
Level Three
Level Four

For more information and a copy of our
prospectus, call Lydia Green on 01742
93921.

Aim for completion in **5** minutes.

Notice 4 | Key in the following notice as shown.

Bright Holidays

Bright Holidays plc are specialists in touring holidays.

Our luxury, fully-fitted coaches allow you to completely relax and enjoy the scenery. Our experienced and friendly tour guides will ensure your holiday is stress free and very enjoyable.

We can offer touring holidays in a number of destinations. A few of which are shown below:

France
Italy
Spain
Lake District

For further details call Mr V Eccles on 01986 382910.

Aim for completion in **10** minutes.

Notice 5   Key in the following notice and add emphasis.

Countryside kitchens

We are experts in designing and fitting high-quality kitchens.

We can help you to plan the kitchen of your dreams no matter how big or small.

Countryside kitchens are also suppliers of:

Cookers
Dishwashers
Fridges
Freezers.

Write or telephone us for a free brochure and details of our kitchen planning service.

Aim for completion in **5** minutes.

Notice 6   Key in the following notice as shown.

THE TROPICAL LEISURE CENTRE

wishes to recruit a

DEPUTY MANAGER

to assist the Manager in the smooth running of the Centre.

Applicants should hold relevant qualifications and have had at least 3 years experience in supervisory management.

Benefits include:

25 days paid holiday
Generous relocation package
Competitive salary

*Write to Joyce Hill enclosing a copy of your
Curriculum Vitae by 28 July.*

Aim for completion in **10** minutes.